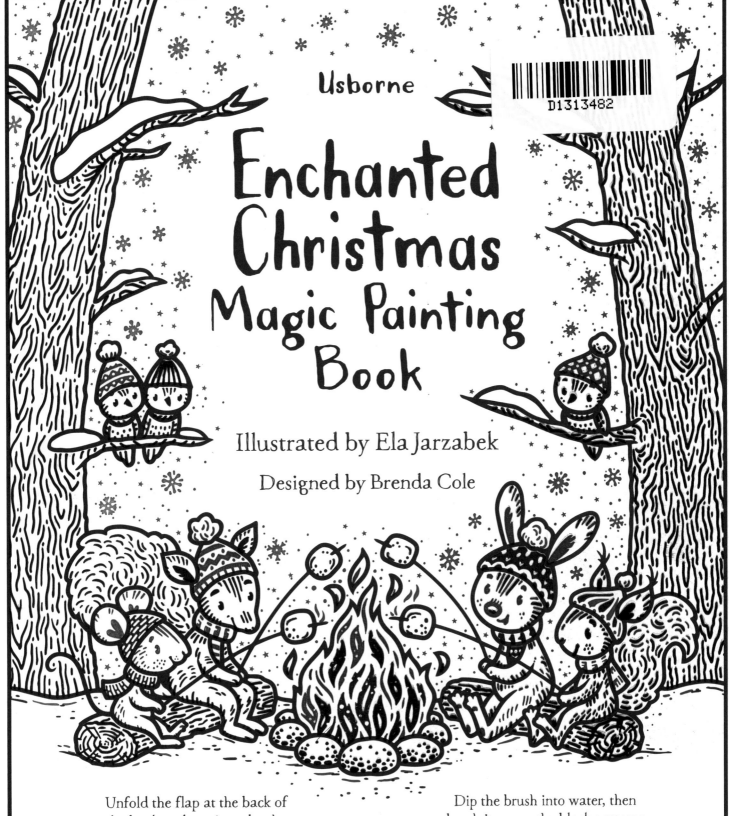

Usborne

Enchanted Christmas Magic Painting Book

Illustrated by Ela Jarzabek

Designed by Brenda Cole

Unfold the flap at the back of the book and put it under the page you're about to work on. This stops water from seeping through onto the next page.

Dip the brush into water, then brush it across the black patterns within each shape to see the paint magically appear. Wash the brush before you paint each new shape.

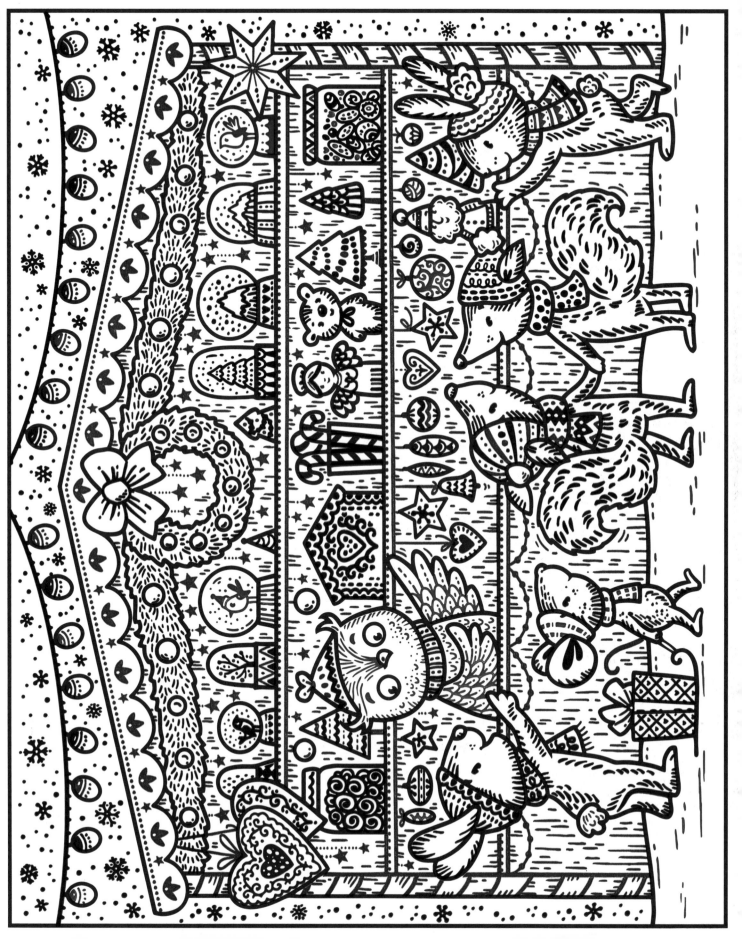